BILL & HILLARY'S

LITTLE BOOK OF

PROMISES

Written and Compiled by Dave & Sharon Robie

STARBURST PUBLISHERS™

P.O. Box 4123, Lancaster, Pennsylvania 17604

To schedule author appearances write:
Author appearances, Starburst Promotions, P.O. Box 4123.
Lancaster, Pennsylvania 17604 or call (717) 293-0939.

Credits:

Cover art and Illustrations by Bill Dussinger.
In Case You Forgot! adapted from "Clinton, After Raising Hopes, Now Tries to Lower Expectations,"
    New York Times, 11/9/92.

We, the Publisher and Authors, declare that to the best of our knowledge all material
(quoted or not) contained herein is accurate, and we shall not be held liable for the same.

First Printing, September 1996

ISBN: 0-914984-90-X
Library of Congress Catalog Number 96-70116
Printed in the United States of America.

Over 5,000 years ago,
Moses said to the children of Israel,
"Pick up your shovels,
mount your asses and camels,
and I will lead you to the promised land."

Nearly 5,000 years later,
Roosevelt said,
"Lay down your shovels,
sit on your asses, light up a camel,
this Is the promised land."

Now,
Bill Clinton is going to
steal your shovels,
kick your asses, raise the price of camels,
and mortgage the promised land.

Whitewater ain't over
'til the First Lady sings.

If it doesn't add up,
change the numbers!

Hillary's Bestselling Books
The Submissive Woman
How to Stay Out of Jail—
Self Help for Felons

Bill's Bestselling Books
Life During Wartime
To Tell the Truth
Unshakeable Principles I Live By

"One for you, Two for me."

In Case You Forgot!

Bill promised to end welfare
"as we know it."

Bill's Friends in High Places

Zoë Baird & Kimba Wood
Failed nominations

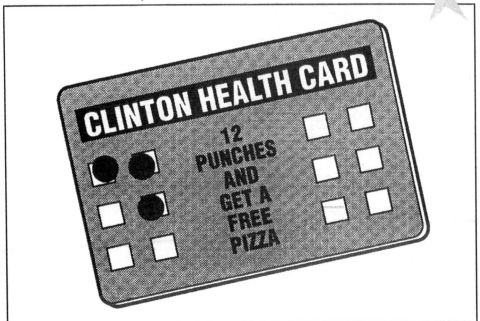

Hillary's Imaginary Friends
Eleanor Roosevelt
Gandhi

If Hillary can have
imaginary friends,
why can't I?

Bill's Imaginary Friends
Pamela Anderson *(Baywatch)*
Heather Locklear

Bill's Cameo Appearances on TV
Murphy Brown, The X Files, Love Connection and *Unsolved Mysteries*

Hillary's
Hair

The Marge Simpson

Clinton's Favorite Wartime Song
Over Here

What travel agent
did you say you use!

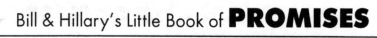

Bill's First Feature Film
Waiting to Inhale

Bill's First Animated Film
The Lyin' King

Bill's Favorite Bible Verse

Render unto Caesar that which is Caesar's.

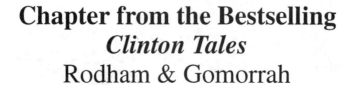

Chapter from the Bestselling
Clinton Tales
Rodham & Gomorrah

George Bush—
No new taxes!

Bill Clinton—
No! New taxes!

In Case You Forgot!

Bill promised to restore America's industrial manufacturing base so that good, high-paying jobs are widespread.

George Bush—
Read my lips.

Bill Clinton—
Read Hillary's lips.

Bill's Friends in High Places

David Watkins (White House Director of Administration)
Resigned—Travel Office fiasco and
used a Marine helicopter to go golfing

Hillary's
Hair

The Whoopi Goldberg

We decided to place a statue
of Bill Clinton beside the statue
of Christopher Columbus, the
greatest Democrat of all time . . .

He left for the New World not knowing where he was going, did not know where he was, returned not knowing where he had been, and did it all on borrowed money.

All roads lead to
Whitewater . . . errr
White House?

My owner is three fries short of a
Happy Meal.

**Hillary's Favorite Saying
to her White House Staff**
Okey-dokey, artichokey!

Favorite Songs
George Bush—
God Bless the USA
Bill Clinton—
To All the Girls I've Loved Before

In Case You Forgot!

Bill promised to insure that no working family would fall below the poverty line.

New White House Dance Craze

Take 2 steps back, spin,
1 step forward, grin,
do the Clinton.

Bill on Balancing the Budget
If I get elected for another 4 years, I'll
have enough to retire.

Bill & Hillary's Little Book of **PROMISES**

When in doubt, say
"I don't remember."

Bill's Friends in High Places

Jocelyn Elders (Surgeon General)
Resigned—inappropriate opinions on
teaching "human sexuality"

Hillary's Nicknames
Wicked Witch of the West Wing
Hilla the Hun

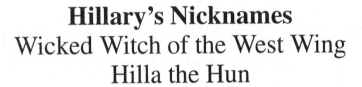

Bill's Nicknames
Wilhelm Von TaxUndSpendenHeim
Bilhelm HotAirenHof
Dollar Bill
McPresident

In Case You Forgot!

Bill promised to make "health care a right, not a privilege," for all Americans without subjecting businesses to an additional tax burden or rationing health care.

Hillary's
Hair

The Dr. Joyce Brothers

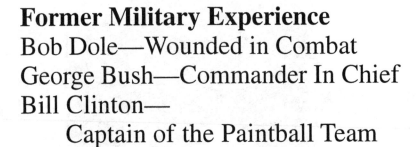

Former Military Experience
Bob Dole—Wounded in Combat
George Bush—Commander In Chief
Bill Clinton—
    Captain of the Paintball Team

Closest Brush with Death
Bob Dole—Wounded in WWII
George Bush—Shot down in WWII
Bill Clinton—Hillary came home early

Autobiographies
Dan Quayle—*Standing Firm*
Bill Clinton—*Hanging Loose*

Bill & Hillary's Little Book of **PROMISES**

Clinton Economics
Farfromthinkin

Bill's Favorite Food
The Waffle

I am glad I am an American.
I am glad I am free.
But, I wish I was a dog,
and Bill Clinton was a tree.

Every cat has his day.

McClinton Burger
Twice the price,
half the meat.

Bill's Boyhood Motto
Crime does not pay . . .
as well as politics.

In Case You Forgot!

Bill promised to halve the Federal deficit in four years without raising taxes on the middle class or significantly cutting the Government entitlement programs that account for the bulk of Federal spending.

Hillary's Hair

The Don King

Clinton Economics II
Taxation without
Hesitation

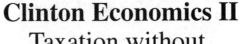

Hillary's New Internet Service
PIP — Psychic Internet Protocol

Hillary's Favorite TV Show
PFN — Psychic Friends Network

What *did* Hillary & Eleanor
talk about?

In Case You Forgot!

Bill promised to eliminate adult illiteracy
in five years.

Bill promised to balance the budget in:

- ☐ a. 4 years
- ☐ b. 5 years
- ☐ c. 6 years
- ☐ d. 8 years.
- ☑ f. All of the above

Bill & Hillary's Little Book of **PROMISES**

Now we pause for a commercial break . . .

Are you out of work?
Do you care?
At the Law Firm of Rodham & Clinton,
we don't care if you've ever put in an
honest day's work in your life.
We think you deserve all the money you
can get, regardless of your ability or
willingness to work.

Bill & Hillary's Little Book of **PROMISES**

Call today, and ask about our "Buy Now and Suffer Later" program. Your first consultation is complimentary. And as an extra bonus, the first 50 callers will receive, absolutely free, a pair of monogrammed rose-colored glasses, and a list of promises not worth the paper they're printed on.

So if you're one of the "motivationally challenged" and want to get what you feel is coming to you, don't wait.
Call today!

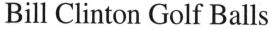

Bill Clinton Golf Balls

They don't fly straight but they
sure give a great lie.

Bill's Favorite Shoes

Flip-Flops

Bill Clinton's Favorite Movie
True Lies

Bill Clinton on Foreign Policy
Back in Arkansas we actually had
neighbors that were from Brooklyn.

Clinton
The best friend
money can buy.

When Clinton said he was going to create
8 million new jobs, I didn't think they all
were going to be tax collectors.
—Jay Leno

Getting Tough on Crime

In Case You Forgot!

 to offer a modest tax break to the middle class.

Rockin' and Rollin' at the White House
*Hillary wants her money for nothin'
and Bill wants his chicks for free!*

It Takes a
Government to *raze*
a Village.

Money Clip of the '90s

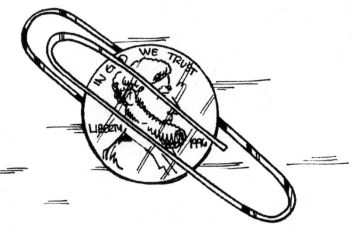

(Penny in a paper clip)

Hillary says...

When in doubt,
do what Bill does . . .
Guess!

New Presidential Theme Song
Inhale to the Chief

When asked about his complete
economic plan, Clinton said that
Socks ate it.

Clinton's War on Crime
Since I came to Washington, crime & drug abuse have dropped in all parts of our United States, especially in Arkansas.

Hillary's Hair

The Eleanor Roosevelt

Bill's Friends in High Places

The late Vince Foster (White House Deputy Counsel)
Died mysteriously

Bill says...

When I want to know
what America
thinks, I'll ask myself!

Bill & Hillary's Little Book of **PROMISES**

Votes for the National Bird
Benjamin Franklin—Wild Turkey
George Washington—Bald Eagle
Bill Clinton—Tyson Chicken

Bill's Greatest Achievements

Then again, you always
get what you pay for.

In Case You Forgot!

Bill promised to keep abortion legal while "making it as rare as possible."

Clip-On
President

Clinton's Re-Election Slogan
OK, this time I'm Really Serious.

School Prayer? But Daddy, kids barely have enough time now to distribute the condoms, stash the drugs, and hide the guns in their lockers.

The Clinton Health Plan is the:
Simplicity of the IRS (Internal Revenue Service)
Efficiency of the USPS (United States Postal Service)
Bureaucracy of the DOA (Department of Agriculture)
Result of Rent Control

Bill and Hillary switched
from MCI to AT&T. They didn't have
enough friends and family to keep up the
calling circle.

If Men are from Mars and Women are from Venus, then Bill must be from Oz.

Grammy Award—
Best New Governmental Artist

Baby Give It Back
by Sir-Tax-a-Lot

For someone who didn't inhale, Bill sure blows alot of smoke.

Hillary's Hair

The Captain Picard
(Star Trek—The Next Generation)

In Case You Forgot!

Bill promised to guarantee all Americans either a college education or two years of vocational school after high school . . . that would "solve the problems of this country while educating a generation of Americans."

Bill & Hillary
They've got what it takes
to take what you've got!

Rodhamhood
She steals from everyone to give to the government.

Bill's Friends in High Places

Bernard Nussbaum (White House Counsel)
Resigned—accused of mishandling
investigative information

If Hillary gets indicted does that mean
Bill becomes President?

I heard
Hillary say to Bill...

My subpoena is
bigger than your
subpoena!

Hoover—Promised a chicken in every pot
Clinton—An unpromising chicken
      who smoked pot

The White House just bought
a $700 toilet seat:

The all new ~~Johnnie-on-the-Spot~~

Billie-on-the-Pot.

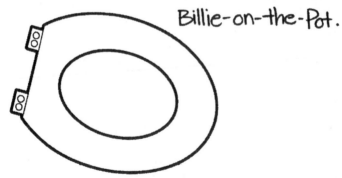

When Bill promised change for America,
who knew he meant he would be
changing HIS position on every issue?

Inaugural Party Themes
  1. A New Day
  2. A New Dawn
  3. A New Pair of Socks

Clinton
Promises Change & Changes Promises

Hillary's Hair

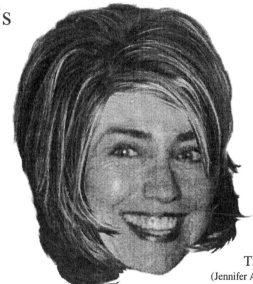

The Rachel
(Jennifer Aniston from *Friends*)

In Case You Forgot!

Bill promised to end racial, religious, geographical, and sex-oriented divisions in society.

Have you heard about the new Bill Clinton doll?

You pull the string and it never tells the same story twice.

Hillary's Quickie Investment Plan
$1,000 = $100,000

First Lady's Pet Projects
1. Education
2. Teen Pregnancy
3. White House Rose Garden topiary
4. Proper support undergarments for the women of Third World Nations

Bill's Friends in High Places

Frederico Peña (Transportation Secretary)
Denver Airport boondoggle while
under his leadership as Mayor

Candid Photo from Presidential Inauguration

Bill's New Campaign Slogan
Maybe I'll get it right this time!

In Case You Forgot!

Bill promised to protect the rights and privileges of workers without costing business growth.

New White House Slogan
"Stupid is as stupid does."

It Takes a Village
(to raise an idiot)

Ok, jokes over.
Bring back Bush!

The higher the
monkey climbs
up the tree, the
more you see his
ugly side.

Clinton Savings Plan
A penny saved is a
governmental oversight.

Hillary's
Hair

The Pippi
Longstocking

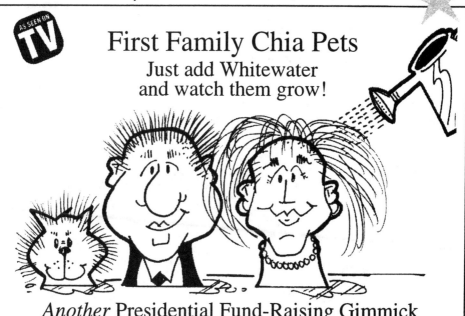

AS SEEN ON TV

First Family Chia Pets
Just add Whitewater
and watch them grow!

Another Presidential Fund-Raising Gimmick

In Case You Forgot!

Bill promised to safeguard environmental concerns without costing jobs.

Second Cousins—Twice Removed

Hillary Rod~~man~~ (ham) and
Dennis Rodman

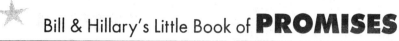

Whitewater Annual Awards
Bill & Hillary voted "Realtors of the Year"

Bill's New Car
The Dodge Drafter

Bill
says...

If at first you don't
succeed, change
your mind!

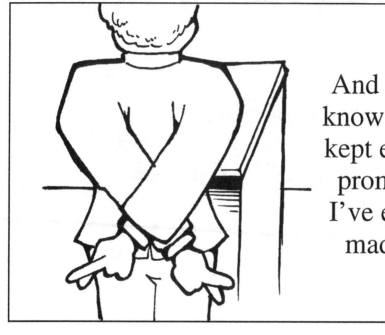

Listen in on Hillary's actual
conversations with Eleanor—
just call **1-800-HILLARY**.

Hillary's
Hair

Ever notice how married couples
start to look alike?

In Case You Forgot!

And now Bill's trying to do it all
right before Election '96!

Bill's Friends in High Places

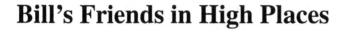

Jack Kevorkian for Surgeon General